Foreword

Throughout the ages, music has been written to inspire and to heightened experience. Much of this music has since been bo: other, equally inspiring occasions where people come togethe. without singing and every set of supporters will at some time feel compelled to join in a communal sing-a-long. Songs may be well known, adapted or improvised on the spot. Whatever the sport or event, it is unlikely to occur without at least some musical accompaniment, proving the irrepressible power of the singing voice. This collection brings together three such wonderful and inspiring songs, which have been adopted by impassioned sporting fans but can also be enjoyed as rousing anthems or encores for any concert programme.

Swing low, sweet chariot started life as a spiritual – it was one of the many religious songs sung by slaves on the cotton plantations in the Southern states of America over a century ago. There has been much speculation as to why it has been adopted by England rugby supporters but it seems that the association is here to stay. This arrangement should be sung calmly but with intensity.

Parry's *Jerusalem* has long been one of the nation's favourite hymns and is a regular feature of any 'Last Night of the Proms' performance (on hearing the orchestrated version by Edward Elgar, King George V said that he would prefer *Jerusalem* to replace *God Save the King* as the National Anthem). Since its creation it has been adopted by many as the official or unofficial anthem of their cause (summer 2005 saw the hymn come to prominence in a new context – this time as accompaniment to the England cricket team's momentous Ashes victory). Here, the arrangement builds steadily over two verses to its powerful climax – enjoy the soaring melody.

You'll Never Walk Alone originally comes from the Rodgers and Hammerstein musical, *Carousel*. It was covered in the 1960s by Mersey group Gerry and the Pacemakers. For a Liverpool supporter, there is little more stirring than hearing fans inspiring their team to greater heights by singing this song. This arrangement represents a unique blend of Rodgers with J. S. Bach. The initial Sondheim-esque piano figures gradually start to feel like a Bach Prelude (rather in the manner of Schubert's *Ave Maria*) and there are other musical quotes included – an *Air on a G string* bass line and an excerpt from *Jesu, Joy of Man's Desiring*. However, none of this should eclipse the power of Rodgers' original melody, which should be sung throughout with 'religious fervour' – long legato lines are the key.

Whatever the histories and contexts of these anthems, it is important to remember that they are designed to inspire. How ever you choose to perform them, as long as your audience members feel the hairs stand on the back of their necks your work is done. Good luck!

Patrick Gazard, May 2006

Editorial notes

Choral basics has been devised to provide arrangements and original pieces specifically for beginner choirs.

Vocal ranges: the arrangements don't explore the extremes of the voice, but aim to stretch the vocal range from time to time in the context of a well-placed musical phrase. Small notes indicate optional alternatives: 1) where the main notes may fall out of comfortable range for some singers, 2) where certain singers on the male-voice part, which mainly falls in the baritone range of a 10th (B–D), wish to explore the tenor or bass register, or 3) where doubling within a part is suggested.

Breathing: singers should aim to follow the punctuation of the text and breathe accordingly. However, commas above the music suggest places to breathe where not provided for within the text.

Piano accompaniments: the simple yet imaginative piano parts have been written to support the vocal lines. Small notes in the piano part are intended to help support singers while learning the piece; however, once more confident you may choose to omit the notes, or just to play them very gently.

Swing low, sweet chariot

Spiritual
arr. Patrick Gazard

Calm and smooth, but keep moving ♩ = 104

6

Moving on a little

con Ped.

con Ped.

Jerusalem

William Blake (1757–1827)

C. H. H. Parry (1848–1918)
arr. Patrick Gazard

And did those feet in an-cient_ time Walk up - on

Eng - land's moun - tains green? And was the ho - ly Lamb of _ God On Eng - land's pleasant pastures seen? And did the Countenance Divine Shine forth upon our clouded hills? And was Jerusalem builded here Among these dark Satanic mills?

You'll never walk alone

from *Carousel*

Oscar Hammerstein II (1895–1960)

Richard Rodgers (1902–79)
arr. Patrick Gazard

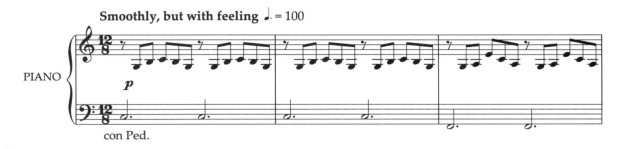

lark._____ Walk on through the wind, Walk on through the rain, Though your dreams be tossed and blown.